Eyes Are Notorious

First published in India in 2024 by CinnamonTeal Design and Publishing

Copyright © 2024 Sipra Roy (Urmila)

ISBN: 978–93–93984–53–1

BISAC: POE000000/POETRY/General

Cover Painting: Author

Butterfly element artwork: image by freepik

Typesetting and Cover design: CinnamonTeal Design and Publishing

CinnamonTeal Design and Publishing
Plot No 16, Housing Board Colony
Gogol, Margao
Goa 403601 India
www.cinnamonteal.in

Eyes Are Notorious

URMILA

CINNAMONTEAL
DESIGN & PUBLISHING

The author with her husband the late Pranab Kumar Roy during the 60s.

Dedicated to my husband, the late Pranab Kumar Roy.
(Born – March 18, 1940 in Plassey, West Bengal)
(Died – March 6, 2001, in Calcutta)

Contents

Eyes Are Notorious! – Part 1

Eyes are notorious
As eyes opened, all creatures
Became predators to each other
'Eat or be eaten' that
Predicts Darwin's doctrine!

Innocence evaporates as the eyes set in
They allured man to commit the First Sin,
Without them neither apple nor snake
Would have been seen!
Eyes caused Paradise lost
And exile to this mortal earth,
Eyes are so notorious!

Neo-Canterbury Tales

In this digital age
The new pilgrimage
Rushing in the race
To their Jerusalem,
Which is a temple of Desire
To end the endless hunger
Of getting more and more.

Modern Chaucer, as
Alibaba, Google and others
Are in the new roles of leaders
To sing Canterbury tales
Erupting from the 'www' vale.

Credit cards, debit cards
Stand for new-age stakeholders,
Replacing the role of Middle-age
Cut-throat Knight Templers,
Will the pilgrims come back?
Or spin around the wisp-o-will
Or in the endless maze of mirages;
Or rush just like flocks of flies in the fire!

Some may look behind
The ashes of burnt wishes,
Forming mounds like sand dunes
In the desert of Desire,

                    Urmila

Waiting to be shifted
By the wind, blurring the air!

Blessed are those, who with a puff,
Blow off the heap of ashes,
They achieve the touchstone of wisdom
That it is a myth to get the golden deer
They were chasing long after;
In vain, to quench their thirst of desire!

But pity on those greedy fools who are still
Ready to step the trodden path again,
Forgetting the graveyard of frustration,
Being blind to learn from blunder any lesson;
Such is the myth and mystery of Desire!

New Age Entrepreneur

In the near future
No wonder will remain a wonder,
Wonder will be a norm
Bereft of any "novelty" in form.

Myriad of scattered genius all around
Huddle in an Olympic of intelligentsia,
Either to create an 'inflation' of geniuses
Or for 'inundation' to be wiped out from the
universe!

Now it's time for the Commoners to rise up,
Upon the cemetery of the crushed past.
Expected high tide for the awkward, backward
Who will be promoted to get even the Nobel
Award!

There will be a tough struggle
To own the have-nots and disable,
Who will be the precious capital
For investment in the market for sale?

Very soon, the enthusiastic entrepreneur
May jump to reign the market
To cash on the best opportunity
To crop up artificial disabilities.
The world will be over-crowded
With an abnormal crippled human species!

   Urmila

Slum dogs are upgraded, the dream of greedy billionaires,
The Hollywood–awarded movie is the eye-opener!

NB. The OSCAR awarded movie: "SLUMDOG MILLIONAIRE" by Danny Boyle.

Social Avalanche

Golden days of marriage are by-gone
Now sex is only for fun,
So long a marriage sustains
On the goal of raising a home,
Which is on the verge of bidding farewell.

A shocking shift in the marital landscape,
What happens in America today
The world will follow next.
Unleashed female freedom
Ultimately changed the ethics of the society's
form!

Now children are born outside of marriage
Without social stigma, bold virgins manage.
Willing virgin buys an egg to be a mother,
Borrows from the bank, like clothes or a car!

Babe-business is flourishing in a shopping mall
As a potential living doll, run by a magnate
mogul!
Bank babe, Lab babe, Tube babe and
Babe of a High-ranking company with a brand!

But nobody knows whether
Babes, with or without any brand
Shall become moths, wasps or butterflies,
When in future they become adults!

 Urmila

Without real parents or a family
Yet life will flow in an eroding valley.
Who knows what shape or fate
The future of this human race will get!

In the new demography,
Where to find the biological babe?
Must be coiled in some neglected corner
Of a dark unprivileged 'third world'
Hatching for another spiral evolution!

Conference after conference will be held
To decide which one of the two sets:
'Natural selection' or 'Artificial adaptation'
Will be the fittest to survive,
Awaiting for some new Darwin to decide!

Singularity

Bond of bio-sex knells the bell,
This is the last generation
Of male and female
As their love turns out to be
A burnt out candle!

The new age opens the screen
Of a new emerging gender – 'singularity'.
Singularity is the only answer to the future!

What causes this great fall?
Who will put Humpty-dumpty
Together again?

Nature is no more their cupid
To unite them, as it failed to cope with
The deal or ban the birth-control 'peel'.

The peel shook the marital plinth,
Losing the key of that sacred fidelity,
Which sustained the strength of the age-old
link.

Is there any chance to go back
To the lost pavilion?
To play in the Garden of Eden
For a new start again?

     Urmila

Buds-in-Clasps

Some poems are genuine
From my own heart!
Born like a fountain from the mountain,
While some are created
Like a test-tube babe in the lab.
Some are hybrid, fused with chewed matter,
Old wine in a new bottle, with added flavor.
Now it is hard to decide, which one to invite
To open her veil in the enlightened elites' vale.

The natural shy one may not be shining
Somewhat odd and novice, but very much my
own.
To appear in the publishing house,
Should I deck them with wordy glamor
And modulate with a catchy costume
Or find some mentor to censure the volume?

NO, never!

Rather let them remain as clasped in buds
In my dark cupboard,
Until welcomed by nature
To blossom and spread fragrance in the air!

Art for Art's Sake

Art for art's sake is now quite fake
It is a relic of the by-gone days,
Religion, art or spirituality
Are now traded as a commodity.

It was true before the dawn of civilization,
When men were crawling from cave to forest
To hunt for food and fruits to collect.

The time they learned music from birds and
crickets
And learned dance from the swaying branches
of trees.
Like slim slender bamboo or corny pine
That moves with the wind in their own style.
In rhythm with a mild breeze or wild gale
Or from the leaves shivering in raindrops
Like an untouched young virgin!
And the airy angel carried the fragrance
Of the first rain-soaked earth with cheers;
That time only meant Art for Art's sake!

     Urmila

To compete in the 'survival of the fittest'
Art-world is twined with modern tech,
Our everlasting thirst for novelty thrives
Us to a new–born creative digital world,
Reducing the art and artist to a commercial
product!
Still, traditional art shall eternally live
To fulfill the heart and to feed the thirsty eyes!

Fugitive

They come, the foreign words;
They come in my sleep,
Knock me to wake up.
The words! The captive words rebel,
Spinning, rattling and hurling
Against the wall of my skull.
I hear their noisy call in slumber,
"Get up, please release us,"
I console: "Relax, till the sun is up!"

I recall those nocturnal nutty guests
In my chosen time of rest,
But get no response to my request.
I search them, summon them in vain
I fail to trace them anywhere, far or near.
Lost like a faded echo in the air
Before I trace them in ink and paper.
The white paper stares at me, blank,
My pen lies idle on the wooden plank!
Though I dive deep for those captives
But they prefer to become fugitive!

 Urmila

About The Poem

It is a coincidence that I started writing poetry, and that too, in a foreign language, just after coming to America a couple of years ago.

In the beginning, it was quite hard for me to find suitable words for my verse. Words or ideas always knock at odd hours and vanish from the mind when they are invited earnestly. I stumble upon an idea and fumble for the right words; thus my poem "FUGITIVE" came out. It was my trial, my third or fourth attempt at poetry in English.

Morgue

I wanted to roam in the garden of Flora
To smell the fragrance of the summer flowers,
But I stepped by mistake into a poetry Morgue
Where I saw a cluster of elite bards, not my
familiar.

Sitting in the front of a casket brought by a
poetry mentor,
One by one the poems from the casket
appeared
To those elite judges, who like surgeons
Dissected and diagnosed the lines and words,
Which were torn or plucked from the corpse of
the verse.
To explain the emotion, meaning and theme
Of which the poets themselves were (perhaps)
unaware!

Commentary on the poem "MORGUE"

I believe that 'writing' can be considered a craft, which is permitted to improve or develop; whereas poetry is quite different. It is an emotional outburst, like spring or a geyser, or a volcano (a gift of Nature).

It is an exclusively unique expression of the poet him/herself. There shouldn't be any imitation or Xerox of a particular poet's emotion, which spoils the poet's genuineness.

We can discuss the great poems from the standpoint of inspiration, theme, language, genre, etc. And not manufacture poems in workshops; it will lead us into digging a 'BURIAL' ground for poetry!

Paradise-Downfall to Poetry-Mall

O poetry, the Divine Voice, the Queen of
language!
Why do you stand in the corner with a
veil, hiding your face?
Are you dethroned now?
Where is your past glory or glamor?
Who holds interest in Virgil, Chaucer or Homer?
Once you burst forth from the heart
Like a spring, cracking the hard rock
To release long-suppressed pain and joy
That melted in the flowing stream of eloquent
thoughts!
Like a queen, you reigned, drenched and
quenched
The thirsty hearts, eon after eon,
But now, where is your crown lost?
O thousand-petal lotus!
Flocks of enchanted bees are focused
Out of you and dispersed
Into multiple streams as 'genres'.
Rich in your juicy nectar,
Colored chambers of literature!
Though your luminary has been pale
Poetry-lovers pray for your glorious revival.

 Urmila

In the past, poets were rare
Readers were mostly connoisseurs,
Now heaps of poems lie in vain for readers
Who are scarce! For the new love
That a smartphone captures,
To suck the marrow of emotion
With a flood of information.

Bereft 'E' from the wings of e-motion
New age gives us only motion
That delivers poems like casino-coins
Waiting earnestly for the readers' attention!

Like autumn leaves, millions of unread poems
Are lost in the whirling wind to nowhere land.
Do any of them reach the altar
Of Shelly, Byron, Keats or Wordsworth?
Whose poems are long-lasting in a reader's
mind,
Not momentary as dewdrops
To vanish instantly in the sunlight!

As in some sleepless solitary night,
 A paramour tiptoes to unfurl
The veiled face of an ex-fiancée in Harem.
The poet turns to revisit the pages of his own
poem,
Either to cajole himself or to sigh in silence!

So, poetry of the New Age, what future you
desire?
Hanging on AI or a mind with vibrating
emotions
That inspires images of true love, loss or
romance.
Most modern poems seem to come out
From manufactured selves, like gadgets,
Eager to be marketed as commercial products!
Still, let us hope, Time will bring back
Your crown, your throne!

 Urmila

Poets Are Not Athletes

Poets are not athletes like swimmers,
Or participants in a marathon race.
Tricky as polo players or crazy
Sumo-wrestlers having least grace!
Poems emerge from the depth of the heart
Like a thousand-petal lotus that
Attracts the bees with its beauty and
Sweet fragrance to collect honey.

Poets are fueled by sheer emotion
Not pushed by speed or reaction,
All sorts of art and creativity
Are rooted in spirituality.
Speed is the monster-killer,
A juggernaut to ruin creativity!
We must check the spread of 'SMS' to save
poetry,
TikTok /Instagram aims to charge motion
By sabotaging or berating the 'E' from
e-motion,
Speed of AI will drive literature into a dark
dungeon.

Poetry Workshop

Poetry Workshop? What is that?
'Workshop' in my concept,
Related only to industry or factory,
Mismatched with an emotional product like
poetry!
Out of curiosity, I ventured to enter
Some poetry workshop,
Where participants were mostly
Senior women led by some pastor.
The group shared their creative pieces –
fragments of memory,
Which contained mostly lots of sorrow, tears
and disease.

Urmila

Why memory of aging spins around failures
Not so much on achievements, love or
romance?
And rarely nests on fun, feast or glamor.
Fragments of memory drop like dry autumn
leaves
Though with a patch of yellow, orange, gold or
green!
Journey from youth towards age, similar as
sunrise to sunset.
Looking back to the hubris of youth, the
howling-soul laments,
How tragic is that in a twinkle of an eye, life
ends so fast!

Even the Tiny Worm

Relaxing on the commode of the washroom,
I casually glanced at a tiny worm–of–
centimeter,
Moving by the sidewall slowly, like a well-fed
gentleman
Taking an afternoon walk in the spring season.
Neither head nor tail could be identified from
its body,
But I guessed its head from the direction it was
moving.

Within a few moments, I recognized the worm,
I saw it in 60 minutes of a TV show; its habitat,
two hundred miles deep
In African goldmines, where the
scientists flocked, not for a gold brick
But to collect from the layers of the mines, this
specific species
Who survived for more than five thousand
years, without air,
Water or sunlight! The scientists were
captivated while collecting
The sample of this worm from the walls of the
mines, wondering
How do they proliferate without food, air or
sunlight?

 Urmila

"The worm may proliferate!" startled me: "so I must kill it."
All of a sudden, like a marathon participant, it darted and vanished
Somewhere in the thread-like line between the floor and wall!
I was bewildered at how the message of my perilous thought
Was received by the tiny species?
Are we all connected and covered in the atmosphere
Of wireless "One Consciousness" truly matters!

Mystic Realm

Memory, a crafty device of the mind
with mysticism
Captures the events of moments from flowing
time
And treasures invisible pictures in the secret
chamber of the mind.
What a unique divine gift! Nobody can steal or
shift,
Prince or pauper, all can equally treasure,
invisible to others.
Relishing the luxury of leisure,
Basking on those that inspire,
And ruminating on fond memories,
Defying the irresistible time
One can roam back and forth in memory lane!
Time, despite being so powerful, is imprisoned
To any mind, whether strong or fragile!
Some memories surge with sensual appeal
Some lark in the dark, while some slip or flee,
Only episodic emotional moments
Spur flush-bulb memories!
But sweet or bitter, doesn't matter
As I glimpse like an onlooker.

 Urmila

Ecstasy of joy, scorching pain or malignant
malice
All softened through the passage of time
What remains is mostly metamorphosis!
Blessed are the humans with memory-as-
portable Paradise!

Last Stop

Every beginning is followed by a closing
ceremony,
Boom and bust regulate overall destiny.
It pervades in every speck of the earth,
All phenomena come under the same physical
path.

In the prohibited Garden of Eden,
Information technology is the latest dragon.
Instead of a single bite (byte),
The whole apple has been swallowed.

Future generations with a barren brain,
Need to borrow from the Internet
Whatever they need to know!
What seed is left after the global rampage
For the future species as a product of
knowledge?

Where to seek the holy seed?
At the North Pole Svalvad or Microsoft Github?
What will happen if it is destroyed by a raging
comet?

Will our beloved planet be the empire of
Sphinx, Chimera
Or be ruled by some alien from another planet?
Will the story of Adam, Eve and the snake
Finally take refuge only in the Bible's page!

Mocking Fish

It was our Sunday delicacy at lunch,
A dish of whole butterfly Branzino fish
With cauliflower, carrot and green peas.
I was happy saving money by avoiding a
restaurant
With an added cost of taxi tips and time.
Though the fish in 'Whole Foods' are well-
cleaned,
Still as a typical Indian lady, I can't but put it
again
Under the tap of the kitchen sink.
I put it under the tap water to clean
Thoroughly, through the tunnel of an opened
mouth!

As ill luck it would have been,
The tongue of a fish was seen
I reviewed a second time to become sanguine,
It was exactly like a human baby of one month!
Repulsively I tried to shut its mouth
But no doubt, it was too obstinate to obey me!

 Urmila

I put it on the pan in hot oil and as I turned it
The silly funky fish sprang out its longer
tongue,
(Reminded me of wanton boys of the drop-outs
school gang)
The mockery of a dead fish from the frying
pan,
Capable of spoiling our fun
Of enjoying our Sunday delicacy for lunch!

Spirit of Icarus

Icarus! Your spirit is ever-lived,
Your immortal vive is imbibed
In the flowing blood of your successors
Who out of your ashes appeared as Phoenix
birds!

Millions of miraculous illumined minds,
With juvenile vigor and immense power,
With new app, AI and sunscreen cosmic attire,
Spirit of Icarus is vibrant in the new generation
They are modeling a rest-room in a space
station!

They are no longer mythical figures!
To unfurl the mystery layer by layer,
Racing far beyond the global horizon
Not to a land of Utopian fantasy, but
Attempting to achieve the unachievable,
With a dream to clean and cool the ozone layer,
(Where to encroach or anchor, even the devils
dare not to go too near).

For saving Mother Earth from the global warm!
Icarus! Your unfulfilled wish is revealing as
glorious!!

 Urmila

Icarus was a young boy from Greek Mythology. His father made him wings and attached them to his back using wax. He warned Icarus not go too near the sun because it would melt the wax, which may lead to his death. In spite of this, Icarus flew too high, near the sun, ignoring his father's warning and turned into ashes. So, curiosity alone kills not the cat but ambition or limitless passion is also a danger to humanity. Icarus is considered a metaphor for human ambition!

Myth of the Crow
Part-1

The funeral was over, the mourning party left,
Me alone, emptiness and the flat.
I woke up early, as usual, before the birds
chirped
But lay on the bed, aware, but with eyes closed.

I heard the chatter of the morning walkers
Louder than the chorus of the morning crows,
The sound of the opening shutters of shops and
garages,
Doorbell by the milkman, newspapers and horn
of the school pickups.

Blow of the conch and smell of burnt incense
from the neighbors
Reminded me that it was 'Holy Thursday'!
I caught all nuances of sound and smell,
Of which, I was unaware for the last three
weeks.

Getting up, as I opened the door of my balcony
I noticed that the soft glow of the morning sun
was sweeping in,
Cool fresh air brushed my face,
Everything around the neighborhood
Was surprisingly the same, with no change!

 Urmila

Coming inside with a somewhat vacant mind
I followed the habitual routine like a machine,
Sat on the balcony with a cup of morning tea,
No sooner, a crow perched close to me.

I kept a piece of toast on the grill,
(So that it left me alone) but it
Neither moved nor touched the toast,
Instead sat fearless and indignant
Until I finished my tea.

Next couple of days also it came,
Suddenly it flashed in my mind,
Can it be true that the deceased soul
Revisits the abode as a bird or pet?

Myth of the Crow
Part-2

One morning, to my fun, I heard a 'caw-caw',
As if querying me, "Why are you so late?"
Keeping the tray aside, I took a biscuit
While another crow joined the tea party.
I was confused, deciding among these two
Who was the spirit of my deceased husband?

First time in my life I noticed
These scavengers are not
As ugly as we think.
Their bodies were shiny and clean,
Eyes were as bright as beads!

The thin younger one might be a female,
However, I divided the biscuit for them both.
The regular fat one declared, "Caw, caw,"
Perhaps to mean, "The introduction is over, let
us go!"

They picked up their own share and flew away,
Gazing at their joyful parting I thought,
How smart are you to pick up your partner
So soon in the other world too!

 Urmila

Spirit in Silence

What can be more eloquent than silence
In the vessel of any language?
However delicate or complicated,
Language is designed to be
An external apparel or costume of feeling!

Feelings are too subtle to be exposed
In any vehicle of language.
More the feeling goes profound,
More the speech loses its sound
Becoming dumb but super-sensitive,
Like the primitive one of the by-gone days.

Love, hate, jealousy or fear
All suppressed, hidden, unspoken words,
Reflect messages either in the eyes
Or in body gestures!
Just as do the innocent animals.

In the vessel of language
Nothing is more eloquent
Than the spirit- in-silence!
Deep meditation is always
In speechless consciousness.

Unsung Part

Aging is the most unsung part of life,
All over the world, humans cling to vibrant
youth
Wrinkled skin, hair gray and thin, pain in the
knee,
Short of hearing, loss of teeth and dim eyesight
With lots of changes in appearance, nobody
invites aging;
Physical and mental frailty cause depression,
Dementia, Alzheimer's, a plethora of disorders,
What more can I add to mention?

But we often forget to count the positive side of
aging,
Great relief from the responsibility of family
raising,
Government support of food stamps, medical
insurance
And senior concession in a subway train or
metro bus;
Sometimes, even the entertainment door is
open at a cheaper price!
As the body weakens, our sensitive inner-self
awakens,
We dive deep and find hidden treasures of our
own,

 Urmila

Not the earthly treasures, but the ever-eternal creative zone;
Uncared and neglected as fallow land for life long!

Why?

Why aging turns us like plants of autumn,
Slightest sentimental touch causes
To shed fragments of memory as dry leaves,
Either piled on or blown by the wind to ditches
To convey only a message of loss and sorrow!

If variety is the spice of life
Why not the memoir of elders too be?
Where did the glory of the past, the story of
romance fly?
Are they gone with the wind in an arid desert
To leave a warm sigh and release a hidden tear?

In spite of highlighting the sad, bitter part
Let the aging sprinkle laughter and humor,
To be served as dessert to add some flavor
By vaporizing through the strainer of memoir.

I remember my cute tiny niece
Once fell from a swing and struck her head,
She got up with tearful eyes but pretended
Not to cry and said, "See me, Mom,
I got hurt from falling yet I'm
Not crying."

Perhaps so little yet so strong and great a
lesson,
The psychosomatic difference on the plane of
aging!

Let it Be

Hey, John Lennon!
Did you sing or yell "Let it be?"
By tearing a heart's string,
What an irony!

When the last hope is lost in some blackhole
Beyond control,
Did you burst out crying in agony,
Which outflowed in the melody, "Let it be?"
Or maybe it is a 'self-consoling' symphony!

It is easy to say, "Let it be" but you know,
Hardest thing to follow;
While the crazy mind desires to grab
The desired part of an entire universe!

When the heart howls, "Let me possess
What I wish," How can I sing along
"Let it be?"

It is easy to sail the boat with the wind
Only the cowards feign to camouflage "Let it
be!"
The brave like Socrates, Jesus or Moses
Struggled hard to row against the stormy ocean
As they never surrendered to the situation!

"Let it be" means "I am defeated,"
Indulging destiny to tame and rein
There is no way but to yell and feign,
"Let it be!", "Let it be!"

Graffiti for Whole Food

Long waiting is boring,
Impatience often goes on soaring,
So, leaning against the side railing
I shifted my attention towards 'watching'.
My new discovery, a debut:
The joyride of a face-scanning journey
A voyage in the Whole Food crowd!

Upwards and downwards, two twin escalators,
Sliding with two sets of people
But each in reverse ways;
The loyal machine continually running
Like a movie on the screen,
Most upcoming commuters
Carrying in their hands Whole Food bags,
Have an "all-done" message
Marked on their glowing faces!

Against the background music
Of buzzing noises in multitude,
I click an invisible psycho video
And tweet each shopper a caption
That came by floating in my mind
About each face and body expression!

 Urmila

To the smiling faces, I tweeted,
"Nice, keep on, happy guys,"
The busy faces are tweeted,
"O, I have yet miles to go!"
To the stern faces with frowning eyes,
I tweeted, "Relax babe, relax!"

For the aggressive bully faces,
I cautioned others, "Beware of the Doberman!"
I tweeted for the giggling youth,
"Treasure a bit for the future, you flamboyant!"
To some romantic clinging couple
With desperate exposer to mettle,
I send an SMS, "Can you save
A Nano-dust of your sediment love
Reserved for the bedroom please?"

With the above videos
In all forms of art,
Collage, motif or mural,
I wish to decorate the wall
With the title "Graffiti for Whole Food"
Presented by 'Anonymous'!

Fear

From childhood, we are chased by a monster,
An extremely unpleasant emotion known as
fear!
The monster changes its form like a chameleon,
To encounter different persons in different
stages!
Fear of death, disease, war or natural
calamities,
Capture universally similar as victims of
destiny.
But the phobia of fear is a dark psychological
trap,
To engulf shadow over joy and peace
snatched from life.

In childhood, friends pitched in me the fear of
ghosts;
Teenage worried me to keep up my glory as the
best girl, my father can boast.
I made him happy by being the ideal ,model' in
school and in town!

When my father left me alone in the college
hostel,
With his almost empty money bag, I wept in
silence,
Pressing my face on the window pane, holding
two
Green apples and some notes in my palm, given
by him.
Thinking of his tired sweaty face, which
appeared calm
For being lucky to arrange the best
University hostel for me
That was quite hard to arrange in Calcutta, a
mega-metro city!

Every morning of my college life I woke up,
With the thought, "How had been my dad, mom
and family?"
My father used to suffer from gout and arthritis
from his forties;
Sometimes, I saw him crying in acute pain like
a baby!

With time the memory of the empty money bag
and green apples
Swayed by the new wave of thoughts; I was
taken by
Worry of self-guardianship; though
my friends guarded
Me to drive away the curious boys around me.
I felt nervy, worried but romantic to notice the
silent messages
In the eyes of those pop heroes, but cautious as
they began to follow me.
Surrounded by three friends, I used to move
even
From class to the common room or canteen!
I always tried to avoid them by taking the back
stairs of the college!
I avoided, perhaps in the fear of what to say if
they asked me
To have coffee with them or accompany them
for a matinee!

Coming to the University, I became prominent
on the campus
From the canteen to the Student Union as
confident and courageous,
Tall & slim girl with long hair' but too proud to
converse!

                    Urmila

After the result of my MA, my marriage was fixed by my parent's choice
But a stranger to me! I woke up at midnight to check the W-card,
If the name and title of my would-be-husband is odd!
It assured I won't be teased at least by my friends to be mocked.
It was August in India; the weather was humid, the sky was heavy, cloudy.
I was sad; the sky showered heavily throughout the night on behalf of me!

After fourteen years of my marriage, my father passed away,
My brother took me straight to the burning Ghat where my father lay,
Like a ,marble statue', his lifeless body was surrounded by relatives and friends,
A peaceful face with no sign of pain. I bowed down to his feet,
Not a drop from my eye rolled down, until I noticed the half-open gate
Of my house; the gate was always kept locked by my dad.
The half-open gate, as if, messaged the unfortunate fate of the house.

Inside the house, I saw my bereft mom, time was dusk!
I used to think to leave the earth rather than to live without parents!

I overcame the 'fear of Death' since my father passed away.
Death turned out to be just moving from one room to another closed-door room.
Death of my dad made my idea of the other world comparatively profound.
Now, as age is growing, my latest 'fear' is whether physical frailty
Will cause dependency. I wish to die as an independent,
I calm myself by trusting confidently upon destiny!

Urmila

Broken Heart

Broken heart? A phrase of great literary fallacy
Unless the heart is made of glass, metal or plastic!
Shops, of course, display for Valentine's Day
An array of cards in the gallery,
With the image of an oozing red heart
Pierced by an arrow at the center,
Symbolizes juvenile love, romantic in flavor!
But random use of the image turns it
Cheap, naïve, niche and ridiculous, and
Fails both as ‚creative art' or sustaining romance;
But oozing blood from the wounded heart of ‚true' love
Creates memorable lyrics of a love song to impact life-long!
Does a broken heart stand as a metaphor for intense emotion?

Creation Through Cracks

All new things are born out of cracks and
suffering
Bursting the rock or soil, peeps the new
seedling,
Cracking the eggshell, comes out a birdling,
Tearing the womb, a baby sees the first shining!

Behind every new birth, there is a crack and
pain,
Pain is innate in us; still, it's too hard to shun!
As our conscious spirit lures to eternal craving
For earthly pleasures, and comes back again
and again!

Sunrays reach the earth, breaking the layers of
air,
Spearing the cloud in the sky, lightning
appears,
Rupturing the mountain, a river spurts to
drench the earth,
Music springs, tearing the vocal string but
floats in the ether!

New flourishing ideas pop up, stirring the brain,
A poem springs from the bosom out of pleasure or pain.
Just as the flower blooms, struggling from the clutch of buds!
Emotion, sweet or bitter, rocks and knocks the universe,
All sense organs react and respond if the mind welcomes!

All sounds, from buzzing bees to the Big Bang,
Whether thunder against the cloud or rolling waves against the land,
All are created by a crackle or collision,
Just as light or anything new, surges out of exertion!

Abiding by the laws of nature, life is not an exception!
Life and light both burst out of a boom and bang!

Twitter-in-Mirror

Mirror mirror on the wall, who is prettiest in
the world?'
Twitter, twitter surrounding the ether
Whom you prefer to be your master?
Do you wish to sing in your own voice
Or to record others like a parrot is your choice?
(If you have your own voice at all!)
The message by your mild strike on the
keyboard
Makes others dance or scream, howl and roar.
How long will you imitate the parrot from the
golden cage?
After all, a Cage is a bondage, depriving
freedom,

Whether it is of ugly iron or glittering gold!
Cutting the latch, fly high in the sky to blow
the clarion call,
Not in a lullaby twittering tune, but to charge
the confused mind.
Be aware of the immense power that you can
spell,
Don't give in to yourself as a mere article in the
'auction' sale.
Don't be a deer who behaves crazy by the
smell of Musk;
Unaware that the aroma his own body spells!

                      Urmila

Boomerang

'Knowledge is power' according to the adage
It is a fallacy when wisdom is lost in
knowledge.
Man has the curse of the First Sin
As he indulged in invading
The Forbidden Land, for unfurling
The mystery of nature,
And plundering its treasure
For enjoying material pleasure!

He began to till the ground of physical nature
To gain more and more,
As constantly kicked by greed
He forgot where to stop!
Nature promised to fulfill his need
But not the insatiable greed.

Man challenges every sphere of creation,
Wins layer by layer, from heaven to ocean;
But lost the key to stop global pollution,
It endangered the whole creation!
Some visionary poet predicts: for destruction,
Either fire or ice is the option.
Knowledge, which was once booming,
Now it hits the future as a boomerang!

Trick or Treat

It really happened once
In the small neighborhood of Texas.
Richard came to his far-relative grandma
With his New Yorker friend, Nicholas,
To give his grandma a treat of surprise
By an unexpected sudden visit!

Reaching near, Richard noticed the house was
dark
But it lighted up as soon as the door was
knocked.
Ever-smiling, the grandma welcomed him,
"Why are you so late?"
They asked with masks on their faces.
"Aren't you ready to give us a Treat or Trick?"
"Yes, sure," with a mysterious smile she replied.
Following her up to the dining hall, they
noticed with awe
Arrangement of what a grand party, in this
house he rarely saw.
Food, flowers, the finest crockery and a
pumpkin for decor!
Just then, Richard heard another doorbell;
He saw the neighborhood uncle, Mr. Lockwood,
standing at the front door.
"I came curiously to see who has lighted the
house?"

                           Urmila

He enquired hesitatingly, "How did you get the
sad news?"
Sorrowfully he conveyed, "Mrs. Swift passed
away last evening,
Without any suffering! Just after the cremation
rituals, I am coming now!"

Before leaving, he handed over the house key to
the bewildered Richard,
No sooner, the light went off, keeping the house
in an eerie dark.
Looking back once again at the dark, Richard
came out with Nicholas.
Before locking the door, grandma's pet black
cat
Darted inside the house, on their faces
declaring "Me-own!"

Poets' Corner (Prose Poem)

I went to London in May 2023. There, I visited the long-cherished dreamland, the Poets' Corner', at the Westminster Abbey. It is a graveyard for famous poets whose talent left an ever-lasting celestial fragrance in the literary Eden. I smelled the past as current moments in the stream of Time. From Chaucer, and Spencer to Johnson Dryden, Shakespeare, Milton, Marlow and Dickens, all were gathered in conference, either in statues or portraits with the possession of their tombs. But I witnessed the sacred burial ground more enthusiastically than the living conference, unless I noticed the senseless tourists stepping on those marble floors, inscribed with names in memory of the poets, patriots and brave warriors!

The tower of Poets' Corner witnessed not only the poets but statues and portraits of great men like Einstein and Stephen Hawking, as well as martyrs. Even the courageous journey of anonymous warriors inscribed their bravery on the glazed marble decorating the floor. I stepped with caution, zigzagging on the floor to save each glorious name of the past.

     Urmila

Yes, it is the past for those who could stampede the page of history with feet clad in boots, without a bit of homage in their heart!

For a nasty headache, I decided to come back home. Was I shocked? Or was I shattered? Or too cool and calm to be aggrieved?

It was better if I hadn't ever visited the 'Poets' Corner'! Looking at the streaming crowd of gleeful tourists towards Trafalgar from the glass window of the double-decker bus, I asked myself: "Where is the place of fame and glory, if receiving minds are rare and scarce?"

What was the value of name or fame in life? In what respect is life precious if everything dissolves into dust? So what is the most precious among life, fame, death and dust?

Perhaps it is dust! To quote also the Bible, the same, echo' is heard.

(Haiku)

What originates Haiku!
Perhaps to compress the freedom of emotions
To suffocate in the iron chest or to throw until
grave

 Urmila

Bliss of Solitude

O Solitude!
Let me be your shadow
Or shelter me in you,
So that I can cherish my own silence.
Gazing at my own piece of sky
Captured like a framed picture
Through my own window glass!

Let me pause or ponder
How to hide or wrap up
My undefined melancholy,
Or to wallow in the luxury
Of idle imagination with no boundary!

As I nurture in my own fleeting moods
My unfulfilled budding dreams,
Concealed carefully from others,
Which I love to treasure as precious,
To smell and harp on to be joyous.

If I'm shattered from my own land of creation
By sudden inner disturbances,
As stormy noises out of the calm ocean,
O Solitude! Please be my lighthouse,
To anchor me in your safe Island!

Secret Enemy

I overhaul my life in search of a secret dragon
Who keeps me restless by chasing all along,
I dissect the emotional sphere layer by layer
In the abyss of the solitary lab of my mind,
Surprisingly, detected the larking beasts in me:
hope and fear!

Scary fear as a thorny cactus remains
embracing me,
While at the opposite side of a dark tunnel,
Flickering light of enchanting ‚hope'
mysteriously beckoning,
To allure me by a dream and flame of new life!

Driven by failure, frustration, ambition or
anger,
Bewildered ego is sometimes aggressive but
Mostly submissive, I never struggled to win
over!

 Urmila

I survived by neither courage nor wisdom,
But by surrendering to social culture and
custom,
To mute fear or hope – two opposite forces
Waves of time tackle the battle to keep a
balance.
Like a snail I sheltered
Under the shell of patience!
Sometimes, surrender or patience are the best
weapons
To win over the emotional dragons!

Beauty of Alaska

I lost my heart to the beauty of Alaska,
The native Americans named it Aly-Eska,
Which meant for them 'great land'!
I wonder to think how visionary
Were the ancestors by their instinct
To imagine such a potential name in mind!

Eon after eon, the yellow metal remained
Hidden under the rocky glaciers
Unknown to the universe;
But alas! As the river Yukon
Carried some yellow-nuggets in her bosom
To attract the crazy gold-bees in the land to
flock upon.

Some of them made a fortune,
While most were buried under an avalanche,
In a quest of gold-rush as martyrs
Without leaving any trace for us to search.

 Urmila

To view the White Pass and River Yukon
We, the eager tourists, boarded on
The narrow excursion railroad
Under which the nature laid,
Frozen sepulture of a thousand dead
Who came once from the far land to venture
The way for paving the railroad in this pristine
land.

The sigh of that tragic part of history
Offered by the crew guide to the amateur
tourists
Who were relishing the story with snacks and
coffee!
The history of gold and greed shocked me
With awe and an aching heart, viewed I
Nature's cruelty behind such celestial beauty!

Questions

We are born with a plethora of questions
Most of which are left for future generations.
Throughout the ages, questions spin in the
mental-maze
Why this earth is tilted towards injustice,
And inequality between the poor and rich?

Why the brutality of war still persists?
Apartheid of caste, color, gender and religion
Split the world, bring undesired alienations!
How to face climate change, ecological
contamination,
And a pandemic like Covid-19, shaking the
global plinth?

Poets, philosophers and scientists absorbed in
researching
To bring back a balance in the universe and
predict destiny!
Some are solved, but to brainwash the mass-
mind
The intellectuals shifted their attention
towards aliens
And AI as the future rescuers and to solve
problems!

 Urmila

The age-old questions: "Does God exist", "Who
am I?" now eclipsed by
The new adventure and romance with aliens
and AI!
Bliss of innocence is enjoyed only by the
ignorant
Who are abstained of stirring the brain like a
scrambled egg,
Rest of us? Are hybrid chimeras or a myth of
nutmeg!

(Haiku)

I roamed randomly
To drink the beauty of nature
While I missed to notice in my own backyard
The beauty of a dewdrop that dazzles like a
diamond on a single leaf of grass!

 Urmila

A Species in Exile: Hijras
(Hermaphrodite)

Nobody calls you, yet you come
To greet every new born;
To bless? Or to blame? Creator's fault
For digging another fate in the grave,
It is the fault of the star that
Your body is not well-defined
Why do you have to pay the penalty?

The world knows
That gender is only a fraction of life,
Nature's tricky device
To trail each one's traits!
What answer lies about the rest of life?
What do genders mean in childhood
Or at the end of ebbing youth?

Lots of noises are heard about LGBT
Who have perfect bodies with legal rights
To abide by their own minds.
Not a single voice for you
Throughout the ages, until now,
Men trodded the moon and mars
Dived deep into the bottom of oceans.

But to crack the mystery of your body
There is none!
Instead of mutiny, you are only
A puppet of mockery and destiny!

Hijra, do you have joys and sorrows?
Do you ever wake up from a nightmare
And gaze at the midnight starry sky?
To ask, "Why, why am I so?"
Do you ever wet your pillow with salty water
Or strike your head, lamenting against a brick
wall?

Cry, Hijra, cry!
Cry so fiercely that it pierces the universe
To squeeze the 'Big Bang' back into the
Blackhole
To return a new cosmos, unfolding with
balanced particles.

In the Indian Subcontinent, 'Hijras' are eunuchs — intersex people — the third gender. In my time, they were not accepted in the normal society. They had to live in a special community meant especially for them and used to get a subsidiary from the Indian government. They came under a special constitutional law. Even the police would deny to take action if somebody complained against them. There were a lot of stigmas attached to them.

                    Urmila

Usually, they would wear shocking, bright-colored female clothes with a lot of jewelry and make-up. They often looked ridiculous wearing their feminine dresses on their very masculine figures.

They always moved around in a group with the unusual sounds of clapping and drum beats, dancing, showing vulgarity and singing songs in their hoarse voices. The neighborhood would know of their presence beforehand from their sounds, drum beats and unusual clapping.

They obviously visited every house where a new baby was born. They would dance with the baby in their lap and demand money. It was a 'must'. They left the house after blessing the baby; sometimes after bargaining, if their demand was unreasonable.

I composed this poem long ago, before the two thousand millennium. I still see this community in Mumbai, but don't know whether their status is the same in India or if it has changed after the Supreme Court accorded equal rights to the LGBT community.

Eyes Are Notorious! Part - 2

Are eyes really notorious?

Eyes are so precious!
Thanks to our ancestors
For their blessed blunder
We enjoy the wonders of the universe!
As we get the onus of both
The trees of life and wisdom.

For eyes we are free to fly
In the open sky as a butterfly
To suck the honey and the beauty of the earth,
Not to remain shut as a cocoon
To meet the fate of boiling
As a blind silkworm.

Let god eternally monopolize
His domain of Paradise!
We swear to worship them in temples
And bribe various sacrifices to appease.
Let men carry the Divine curse
"To till the land by his sweat until death"
And carry their "blessed" wrath
To rule and reign this wonderful Earth!

 Urmila

Acknowledgment

I am grateful for the guidance and support from Rama Koneru, author of *God is not Optional* which have been invaluable in my journey as an author.

I wrote most of the poems between 2013 and 2016. After that, I spent two years searching for a way to publish them. I used to be comfortable with a pen and paper. I have more than four hundred and eighty pieces of writing. But it was hard for me to make an 'online submission' without somebody to guide me. I met Rama, who was my god-sent angel. I collected about forty poems out of my scattered collection, with Rama's active help.

I am also grateful to my son, Partha Kumar Roy, my daughter, Paromita Roy and my brother, Utpaul Mazumdar for their moral and inspirational support. I am greatly indebted to my late parents, Urmila and Aniruddha Mazumdar, from whom I inherit the legacy of a love for art, literature and spirituality.

About the author

Sipra Roy, AKA Urmila, was born and brought up in India. After completing an MPhil from the University of Calcutta, India, she served as a teacher in a school for under-privileged students.

She traveled to the US on visits to her children and became a US citizen in 2020. She has done three Elderly courses in the US: Foreign Policy of the US, Jewish Religion and Social and Cultural Evolution of New York from the Fordham University.

Though a teacher by profession, Sipra has been interested in writing as a young schoolgirl. She resumed her literary interest after coming to the US. Her mother tongue or native language is Bengali and English is her second language. She is an active member of the Academy of American Poets, IWWG, Florida State Poetry Association and a participant in the Inter-generational Program in DOROT, a Jewish Senior Center. She has written poems, a novel, memoirs, short stories, non-fiction as well as lyrics and drama-skits, which have been staged successfully under the instructions of Broadway Internees. Some of her 'solo' writing pieces have been published on Amazon.com, SCN, FSPA, and Eber & Wein, but have not been published as a book so far. *Eyes Are Notorious* is her debut publication.

www.ingramcontent.com/pod-product-compliance
Lightning Source LLC
Chambersburg PA
CBHW020748160726
47993CB00006B/2665